GALAPAGOS

GALLERY BOOKS
An Imprint of W. H. Smith Publishers Inc.
112 Madison Avenue
New York City 10016

This edition first published in U.S.
in 1990 by Gallery Books,
an imprint of W.H. Smith Publishers, Inc.
112 Madison Avenue, New York, New York 10016

ISBN 0-8317-9596-4

Printed and bound in Spain

For rights information about the photographs in
this book please contact:

The Image Bank
111 Fifth Avenue, New York, NY 10003

Producer: Solomon M. Skolnick
Writer: Claudia Caruana
Design Concept: Lesley Ehlers
Designer: Ann-Louise Lipman
Editor: Joan E. Ratajack
Production: Valerie Zars
Photo Researcher: Edward Douglas
Assistant Photo Researcher: Robert V. Hale
Editorial Assistant: Carol Raguso

Title page: **The Galápagos Islands
contain more than 55 varieties of birds,
27 of which, including the blue-footed
boobies pictured here, are found only in
the islands. *Opposite:* Unlike the familiar
pelicans often seen swooping down on
docks or following fishing boats, brown
pelicans are more sedentary because food
is easy to obtain in the Galápagos.**

The largest island in the Galápagos archipelago, Isabella, like the other islands, was formed by the lava of ancient volcanoes, including the Darwin Volcano in the distance. *Below:* The islands are usually greenest in the winter, after the arrival of the *El Niño* current at Christmastime.

I magine a 500-pound tortoise munching on a giant cactus or penguins basking in the sun on an island at the equator. Four-foot-long lizards that look like the dragons you remember from your childhood storybooks walk on a stark, moonlike, lava-strewn landscape. Imagine too, birds that swim instead of fly and sunflower-like bushes as tall as telephone poles.

Welcome to the Galápagos (pronounced guh-LAH-puhgoes) Islands, a string of remote, volcanic islands straddling the equator 600 miles off the coast of Ecuador.

What some scientists call a "showcase of evolution" was originally called the Enchanted Islands by early Spanish explorers. Consisting of 13 major islands (five large, eight small) and dozens of small lava islets and reefs, the land mass is approximately 3,000 square miles. These islands, which together constitute one of the most active volcanic sites in the world, are scattered over 17,000 square miles in the Pacific Ocean.

In 1892, four hundred years after Columbus discovered the New World, the Enchanted Islands were renamed Archipiélago de Colón in his honor by Ecuador, which had annexed the islands in 1832. But they are rarely referred to by this name. Most people call them Galápagos, the Spanish word for "tortoises."

This page, top to bottom: **Cormorants in other places have strong wings enabling them to fly, but the flightless cormorants in the Galápagos Islands have developed long necks and beaks for fishing. Two young cormorants dry their stubby wings. Cormorants nest on both Isabella and Fernandina islands. *Overleaf:* Isabella has majestic cliffs overlooking waters where birds such as cormorants fish.**

Scientists theorize that the ancestors of these small Galápagos penguins probably migrated from more southerly locations. *Below:* These are the only penguins that do not live in a polar region.

Above: The sun sets on a giant mangrove in Tortuga Bay, Isabella Island. *Right:* Extensive lava fields cover much of Isabella.

Although the Galápagos were discovered serendipitously in 1535 by the Bishop of Panama, Fray Tomás de Berlanga, who was blown off course during a journey from Panama to Peru, some researchers believe that Incas may have explored the islands much earlier, but there is scant physical evidence of their visits.

It was not until 1570, however, that cartographers first put the archipelago on maps. It was a voyage of discovery almost 300 years after Berlanga's visit that brought to the Galápagos their most famous and perhaps most important visitor: Charles Darwin.

The year was 1835, and Captain Robert FitzRoy and his crew were on a five-year around-the-world journey on H.M.S. *Beagle*. On board was a young, unpaid naturalist whose five-week stop at the Galápagos has become a turning point in the evolution of scientific and philosophic thought.

Visiting at least four of the islands, Darwin collected and classified plant and animal specimens. As might be expected for an island chain as remote as the Galápagos, native flora and fauna were different from those species that had been discovered elsewhere. Today, the islands contain some 55 native birds, 27 of which are found only in the Galápagos, and some of those are found only on one of the islands. At least 900 plant species have been identified and, of these, 200 grow only in the Galápagos. Undoubtedly, there were even more species in Darwin's time that he did not collect and that have since become extinct.

He saw the giant tortoises (*Geochelone elephantopus*), noting that there were differences among them – some had longer necks than others and there was more than one

Preceding page, top: A frigatebird chick stays in its nest under the watchful eye of its mother. *Bottom:* Male frigatebirds display their inflated red pouches to attract females. *This page:* Stark rock formations such as the Darwin Arch can be found on San Cristóbal. *Overleaf:* Leon Dormiodo, another impressive rock formation on San Cristóbal, is better known as Kicker Rock.

Preceding page: Sea lions make their home on San Cristóbal in large colonies. Sea lions are one of five mammal species indigenous to the Galápagos Islands. *This page, right:* It is not unusual for sea lions to frolic with human visitors in the waters surrounding San Cristóbal, the island closest to Ecuador. *Below:* Although generally friendly to others in their group, sea lions can also be rather territorial.

A blue-footed booby guards a chick. *Below:* Blue-footed boobies are indigenous to several of the Galápagos Islands.

shape of shell. He observed that the ones found on islands where there was little water and vegetation had the longer necks. Why could this be?

Darwin was particularly taken with the 43 varieties of finches he saw. He discovered that they, too, differed from island to island. Some had short bills while others had wide ones. Again, why?

Then, there were the cormorants *(Nannopterum harrisi).* In South America and everywhere else where they exist, cormorants fly. But in the Galápagos, they have stubby wings which make flight impossible, and extremely long necks. Again, Darwin had more questions than answers.

Perhaps the most unusual animal he saw was the dragon-like marine iguana *(Amblyrynchus cristatus),* which has a spiny crest and grows to be four feet long.

What could account for such an odd assortment of creatures in the Galápagos and the subtle and some-times stark differences in some species? Darwin puzzled over these questions and his observations and notes led to the formation of the theory of evolution by natural selection, which was made popular in 1859 with the publication of his book *On the Origin of Species.*

He theorized that because living things do not generally create exact duplicates of themselves,

Yellow-crowned night herons, like this one, are frequently found on Genovesa Island. *Below:* This immature bird was hatched from one of four or five blue-green eggs laid in a nest made of sticks.

those changes or mutations can help or hinder them, depending on their environment. The isolation of the Galápagos, plus the hardship of living there meant this: to survive, a plant or animal species had to adapt to the conditions or die out. Such reasoning could account for cormorants who no longer needed strong wings to fly considerable distances for food; rather, they would do better with long necks to fish in the waters around the islands.

The different varieties of tortoises evolved in response to where they lived. Just as the cormorants developed long necks and stubby wings, on islands where water and vegetation were scarce, tortoises developed long necks and saddlebacks to reach plants more easily. On islands having more than one species of tortoise, researchers believe that small, distinct ecosystems were responsible for the differences.

Because there were no large predators and because man did not arrive until the sixteenth century, species that may have been doomed elsewhere could thrive in the Galápagos. Many of the seemingly strange animals, the marine iguana for example, may have been spread over a greater area but survived only in the Galápagos.

How the flora and fauna developed on the Galápagos is a great scientific mystery. Equally puzzling is how all these plants and

animals got to this chain of volcanic islands virtually in the middle of nowhere in the first place. There have been several provocative proposals.

Some researchers believe that at one time the Galápagos could have been one single land mass that sank, leaving only the tops of the volcanoes above water. These are the different islands. Other researchers believe that at one time these volcanic islands were closer to the South American coast but gradually drifted away.

Vegetation probably arrived at the islands in several ways. Spores and seeds may have been dropped from birds flying overhead or could have been blown or floated to the islands. Additionally, many researchers believe that floating islands of driftwood and vegetation carried plant life away from South America to the Galápagos. They may also have carried some animals. These floating islands, as well as the birds overhead, could have had some help from two environmental factors: the Humboldt or Peru current and *El Niño*.

The cool Humboldt current flows north along the coast of Chile and Peru and turns west to the Galápagos. Because of this current, the climate is cooler than one might expect at the equator with coastal temperatures ranging between 70°

Preceding pages: **Although marine iguanas are aquatic, they spend much of their time basking in the sun on the shore.** *This page:* **Lava lizards, which can grow to a foot long, thrive in the desert-like conditions on some of the Galápagos Islands.** *Left:* **This lava lizard hops a ride on a marine iguana.** *Opposite:* **San Cristóbal's green Punta Pitt Trail leads to the ocean.**

Bartolmé, the island slightly southeast of Santiago, is rich in scenery. *Below:* Although the island is inhospitable to most animal and plant life, its stark landscape is attractive to visitors. *Opposite:* From the summit of a nearby volcano, the view of Bartolmé's Pinnacle Rock is breathtaking.

Preceding page: One of the many flamingos in the islands wades in a Santa Cruz lagoon. *This page:* The Galápagos hawk, which is indigenous to the islands, is now an endangered species. *Below:* This Galápagos hawk displays the sharp, curved beak which helps make it a fierce predator.

and 80°. There also is less rain, which occurs between January and March in the Galápagos, than at many other locations on the equator. When southwest winds are strong, material floating from South America can reach the Galápagos within a few weeks. Animals such as the Galápagos penguin *(Spheniscus mendiculus)* and the fur seal *(Arctocephalus galapagoensis)* could have arrived this way.

An equatorial countercurrent, or foil, to the Humboldt Current is *El Niño,* "the Holy Child," so-called because it usually arrives during the Christmas season. This warm current, responsible for stormy weather in the islands during the winter, also could have helped the other flora and fauna to reach the Galápagos.

It was not easy to cross the Pacific to the Galápagos in this manner, so relatively few plants and animals survived the trip. As equally important as which plants and animals made their way here is which ones did not and why. Again, there are several provocative theories. Freshwater animals, such as frogs or salamanders, would not be good candidates for an ocean journey. Their soft skin would

permit the penetration of salt water, which would kill them. They are, therefore, not native to the Galápagos. For the most part, land mammals are also not naturally represented in the Galápagos islands. Notable exceptions are two species of bats, which could have been blown in with one of the currents, and small rodents, which may have come with the floating islands.

Did the lumbering, giant tortoises hop a ride in this fashion? No one is sure, but it is possible that tortoise eggs or young tortoises, which are a mere three inches long at birth, could have been on the floating islands. But there are other questions. Were the original tortoises so big, or did they only become large in the Galápagos because predators were absent? How did they travel to other islands in the chain, or did they travel? How old are the tortoises? Again, no one is quite certain. Curiously, giant tortoises are found in just one other place: remote islands off the African coast.

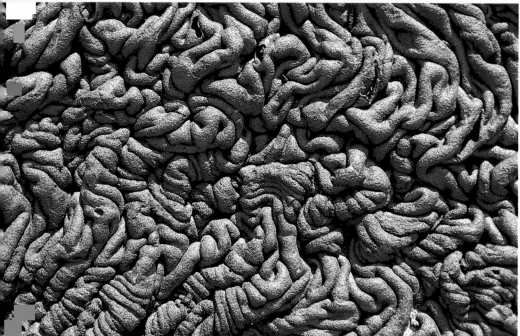

Many visitors to the Galápagos as well as residents did not share Darwin's concern for the environment. Even before Darwin's time, the Galápagos were a haven for pirates and buccaneers. There were fortune-seekers and unscrupulous hunters and whalers. Many who settled on the habitable islands brought with them rude guests: pigs, goats, and dogs, which soon became feral. These animals killed the native animals, destroyed turtle

*This page, top to bottom: **Pahoehoe** lava sometimes hardens into round mounds. Hardened lava may form interesting and complex patterns. These rope-like formations are known as "lava toes."*

This lava field is on Santiago island. *Below: A-a* lava cools rapidly, and is much more jagged than the smooth *Pahoehoe* lava, which cools slowly.

Daphne Island, situated between Santiago and Santa Cruz, is one of the smaller, less-visited islands. *Opposite, top to bottom:* The waters surrounding the Galápagos Islands are a protected marine park where snorkelers can view marine life such as these sea anemones. Sea urchins have a global body covered by spurs. A basket star perches on a sea fan.

eggs, and ruined the natural vegetation. Rats, uninvited passengers on the many ships that stopped at the Galápagos, frequently escaped and inhabited the islands.

Although many native animals have been prey to human greed or indifference, the disappearance of tortoises on the Galápagos is particularly distressing and bespeaks the need for conservation. Zoologists believe that as many as 15 varieties of the tortoises once lived on the islands – 10 on separate islands and five others on Isabella, the largest island. They believe that each of the five on Isabella evolved in isolation on one of the five principal volcanoes that became the present-day island. Today, many tortoises still flourish on this island and on Santa Cruz. Tortoises no longer live on Santa Fe, Rábida, and Floreana islands. On Fernandina, San Cristóbal, Española, Santiago, and Pinta and Marcxhena (two small islands), tortoises are either extinct or close to extinction. What may be the rarest animal in the world is the abingdoni tortoise (*Geochelone elephantopus abingdoni*), found on one of the islands almost 20 years ago.

Even during Darwin's time, tortoises were vanishing from many of the islands. Because tortoises could live for up to a year without food or water, they were treated as "living lunchboxes" by pirates, buccaneers, fortune-seekers, and whaling-ship crews who stopped in the Galápagos to stock up on supplies before returning to sea.

One chilling account recorded in the early 1800's by Captain David Porter, commander of the frigate *Essex*, tells the story. Porter and his crew loaded 14 tons of tortoises onto their ship in four days. Between 1811 and 1844 alone, more than 700 American whaling ships in Pacific waters may have stopped in the Galápagos for

Preceding page: Although by nature retiring, the moray eel will display its teeth if threatened. *This page, above:* A goby cleans the head of a giant hawkfish. *Right:* A brightly colored lizard fish awaits passing prey. *Following pages, left:* The small island of Rábida, south of Santiago, is known for its red sand beaches. It is also home to sea lions, flamingos, and the Galápagos hawk. *Right:* Prickly pear, or opuntia, cacti are usually low-growing bushes, but on Sante Fe they grow as tall as trees.

Preceding page: The land iguana, like many other animals in the Galápagos, has no natural predators and is unafraid of humans. *This page:* This frigatebird chick will eventually lose its white down and grow dark feathers. *Below:* A male frigatebird can inflate its red pouch to about the size of a soccer ball.

The lava-strewn, rocky coast of North Seymour is home to sea lions, frigatebirds, and land iguanas.

North Seymour is also home to this group of blue-footed boobies. *Below:* A majestic great blue heron readies for flight.

supplies. It is a wonder that any tortoises have survived.

The disregard for the natural wonders of the Galápagos would have continued if the Ecuadoran government had not approved legislation in 1934 – 100 years after Darwin's visit – to prevent hunting of native Galápagos species. At the same time, nature reserves were established.

But it was not enough. The laws were not well enforced, and many settlers balked at the restrictions. In 1959, as international environmental concerns swelled, more action was taken: All land not already inhabited (97% of the land mass) was declared a national park. The Charles Darwin Foundation for the Galápagos Islands established a research station on Santa Cruz that year. Since then, the islands have been designated a "World Heritage Site" and a "Man and Biosphere Reserve."

Each major island boasts its own unique ecosystem and geographic features. Although the individual islands were officially renamed in 1892 with the archipelago itself, many of them are referred to by earlier names. Either name or both may appear on a map.

Santa Fe (Barrington) is noted for land iguanas *(Conolophus subcristatus)* and the Galápagos hawk *(Buteo galapagoensis)*. There are also giant opuntia, or prickly-pear, cacti *(Opuntia echios gigantea)* and palo santo trees *(Bursera graveolens)*.

Masked boobies, such as this one on Genovesa Island, have a black face mask around orange eyes. *Left:* A masked booby chick stays close to its mother. *Opposite:* Genovesa Island's Darwin Bay is one of the few nesting places for the red-footed booby.

Preceding page: A lava heron captures a Sally Lightfoot crab. *This page, above:* Swallow-tailed gulls also nest on Genovesa. *Right:* The white spot on the swallow-tailed gull's beak is a sign of adulthood.

Palo santo trees, widespread throughout the islands, shed their leaves during the dry season. *Opposite:* At one time, there may have been as many as 15 varieties of giant tortoises on the Galápagos Islands, but because of unrestricted hunting in the past, few varieties remain.

Above: Although this tortoise is eating, giant tortoises can live for almost a year without food or water. *Left:* Giant tortoises are a mere three inches long when they are born but can weigh up to 500 pounds as adults. *Opposite:* Compared with other varieties of tortoises, the shell of the giant saddleback tortoise is lighter and the neck is longer, making it easier for the giant saddleback to reach and gather food.

Although most of the islands are arid and uninhabitable, Santa Cruz, the site of the Charles Darwin Research Station, has a thick, highland forest and some farms. *Below:* Giant opuntias thrive on Plaza, one of the smaller islands in the Galápagos chain. *Opposite:* Land iguanas are now found primarily on Santa Fe and Fernandina, although they were once widespread throughout the chain.

Plaza's southern cliffs are home to swallow-tailed gulls.

The dragon-like spiny-crested marine iguana is one of the world's most unusual animals and is indigenous to the Galápagos. *Below:* Marine iguanas are at home on land or at sea.

Colorful marine iguanas, which grow up to four feet long, thrive on Punta Suarez on Española. *Below:* Inside the marine iguana's nasal cavities are special glands that remove excess salt in its blood.

Fernandina (Narborough), the westernmost island, has striking volcanoes as well as marine iguanas *(Amblyrhynchus cristatus)*, flightless cormorants, brown pelicans *(Pelecanus ocidentalis)*, and penguins.

Floreana (Charles or Santa Maria) is noted for flamingos *(Phoenicopterus ruber ruber)*, red-footed boobies *(Sula sula)*, and sea turtles *(Chelonia mydas)*, which nest in its dunes.

Española (Hood), the only breeding ground for the waved albatross *(Diomedea irrorata)*, is home for both blue-footed and masked boobies *(Sula nebouxii and S. dactylatra)*, marine iguanas, lava lizards *(Tropidurus grayi)*, sea lions *(Zalophus californianus wollebaeki)*, frigate birds *(Fregata minor)*, and swallow-tailed gulls *(Creagus furcatus)*.

Isabella (Albemarle) is J-shaped with a line of five giant volcanoes. This is the largest island, 70 miles long and 40 miles across at its widest point. Brown pelicans, frigate birds, cormorants, and penguins are found here. Giant scalesia *(Scalesia affinis aster)*, a member of the sunflower family, grows 80 feet tall here.

Santiago (James) has both recent lava flows and hardened black lava. Galápagos hawks, vermilion flycatchers *(Pyrocephalus rubinus)*, flamingos, and fur seals make their homes here.

Punta Suarez is a nesting place for blue-footed and masked boobies, finches, swallow-tailed gulls, lava lizards, and marine iguanas. *Below:* The surf meets the rocky and craggy shore on Española, the most southerly of all the Galápagos Islands.

Galápagos hawks have extremely sharp talons which they use to grasp live prey.

Seymour has sea lions, frigate birds, blue-footed boobies, and land iguanas.

Plaza is really two islands, North and South. It has sea lions, land iguanas, marine iguanas, and red-billed tropic birds *(Phaeton aetreus)*. Large opuntia and other cacti thrive here.

San Cristóbal (Chatham), the island closest to Ecuador, is usually a starting point for inter-island cruising by tourists. The breathtaking rock formation Leon Dormiodo ("sleeping lion"), also called Kicker Rock, is here. Sea lions, blue-footed boobies, marine iguanas, and lava lizards roam this island.

Santa Cruz (Indefatigable) is the home of the Charles Darwin Research Station and a tortoise reserve. This includes a tortoise hatchery, where species from throughout the islands have been hatched. The island has green forests and grassy pampas.

Genovesa (Tower), the most easterly island in the chain, is less than three miles wide. Darwin Bay is one of the few nesting places for the red-footed booby and other birds, including the swallow-tailed gull and yellow-crowned night heron *(Nytenassa violacea)*.

Bartolmé (Sullivan), a small island east of Santiago, has white beaches and volcanic cones but is inhospitable to most animals and plants. Pinnacle Rock can be seen from the cone of one of its volcanoes. Visitors can swim and snorkle here.

Ràbida (Jervis) has red-sand beaches as well as sea lions, flamingos, and Galápagos hawks.

Above: Boobies can dive into the water from steep cliffs to fish. *Left:* A red-footed booby guards a young chick on Genovesa.

Noted for cactus such as this lone opuntia, Floreana is also home to flamingos, red-footed boobies, and sea turtles. *Below:* "The Buccaneer's post office," a remnant from past visitors on Floreana's Post Office Bay, is still used by tourists to mail postcards and letters.

Today, approximately 9,000 people live in small villages and farms on San Cristóbal, Santa Cruz, and Isabella. Baltra (South Seymour Island), north of Santa Cruz, was a U.S. Air Force base during World War II and is now home to a small commercial airport. Santa Cruz also has an airport, but most inter-island travel is by sea. Farming is possible in some areas and some residents raise cattle or fish for a living. Others work in the tourism industry.

With good reason, tourist interest in the Galápagos Islands has mushroomed, but serious problems have burgeoned with this good fortune. Large numbers of tourists can put a serious strain on the islands' natural resources. Unsuspecting tourists may also bring with them unwanted "visitors" such as new strains of virus or bacteria that could destroy the rare plants and animals. On the upside, tourists can help promote the research, education, and conservation efforts in the islands. Although tourism is important economically both to the islands and mainland Ecuador, a careful balance must be struck to preserve the islands. This strategy is sometimes referred to as eco-tourism, and it is accomplished in several ways.

The Ecuadoran National Park Service, for example, limits the number of tourists and requires that all who do visit pay a substantial fee. Along with the Charles Darwin Research Station, the National Park Service has designated 40 visitor sites and made the surrounding waters a marine park. Today, all tours of the Galápagos are led by naturalists certified by the research station.

Without question, the future of the Galápagos Islands and their strange inhabitants depends on international cooperation and a concerted effort to better understand and preserve the delicate ecosystems. A world without giant tortoises, dragon-like lizards, and swimming birds is unthinkable.

Fernandina, the westernmost island in the Galápagos, has active volcanoes and dramatic volcanic scenery. *Left:* Cacti grow in a lava field on Fernandina.

The colorful Sally Lightfoot crab is indigenous to the Galápagos.

The fishing abilities of the Galápagos flightless cormorants are a testament to Darwin's theory of evolution by natural selection, which he formed during his historic visit to the islands.

Index of Photography

TIB indicates The Image Bank